Sharing Our 21st Century

SURVIVE, LIVE, AND THRIVE

SANDY BRÖCKING

First published in 2024

National Library of Australia Cataloguing - in - Publication entry:

Author: Bröcking, Sandy

Subjects: Mind & Body, Popular Works, Poetry, Fiction

Internet addresses given in this book were accurate
at the time it went to press.

Sharing Our 21st Century
Copyright © 2024 by Sandy Bröcking

All rights reserved. No part of this publication may be
reproduced, stored or transmitted, in any form or by any means,
electronic, mechanical, photocopying, recording or otherwise,
without the prior permission of the copyright owner.

This book is based on fiction and is not a substitute for professional or
medical advice and should not be relied on in a place of such advice. Use
of any information contained in this book is done so at the reader's risk.

The author and publisher shall have no liability or
responsibility to any person or entity regarding any loss or
damage incurred, or alleged to have incurred, directly or
indirectly, by the information contained in this book.

Any names or characters, businesses or places, events or incidents
in this book, are fictitious. Any resemblance to actual persons,
living or dead, or actual events is purely coincidental.

Published in Australia

TSW Publishing

ISBN
978-0-6458130-2-9 (Paperback)
978-0-6458130-1-2 (eBook)

We may be right,

we may be wrong,

but an open mind

is what makes us strong.

Table of Contents

Chapter 1 – ABOUT LIFE

Secret 3
Rain 6
Silence Within 7
Precious Things 8
Morning Sun 10

Chapter 2 – OVERCOMING CHALLENGES

Days 15
Keys 17
Miles 18
Buzz 20
Naïve 23
Watching The Wind 26

Chapter 3 – MAKING LIFE EASY

Happiness Goal 31
Life Is 33
One Of Them 36
Stuff Up 38
Trust 39
What's Special About Me 41

Chapter 4 – HEALTH AND KNOW-HOW

Every Day Is A Feast 45
Oh Boy! 47
Betrayed 49
Looking Beyond 52
Never Too Late 55
Growing Old 57

Chapter 5 – A WORLD AROUND US

Happiness Is … 61
Gone Shopping 62
Façade 64
Chaos 67
One Wonders 69
Gold Rush 70
Here 72

Chapter 6 – LESSONS TO LEARN

Thank You, Mum 75
Matters 77
Invasion 79
Lost Season 81
Burned 83
Trojan 85
Unsmart 87

Chapter 7 – IF WE'D ONLY LISTEN

Voices 91
Watch Out 92
Silence 93
Stop 95
Lost 97
Sunrise 98

Chapter 8 – LOVE AND OTHER DILEMMAS

Love 101
Cry 103
Love You All 106
Cherish 108
Don't Miss 110

Chapter 9 – PEOPLE WE MEET

Andrea 113
Life's Pity 115
Ladders 117
Let Go 118
Being Social 119
Loving You 120

Chapter 10 – DOOM, GLOOM, AND POLITICS

Right Or Wrong 125
Cooking The Chef 127
No, Minister 130
Change 132
Bad Luck 135

Chapter 11 – YOU ARE NOT ALONE

Time Of Our Life 139
Alien World 141
Brink 143
Fate 145
Here It Comes 147
Leave Me Alone 149
Fear 150

Chapter 12 – SET UP FOR A WIN

Rest In Peace 153
Free 155
Autumn Leaves 157
Mist 159
Heaven Is Here 160
Lost – Matters 161

Chapter 13 – ESTEEM THE SELF

Being Me 165
Beautiful 167
Is It Me? 168
Women 171
Being Beautiful 173

Chapter 14 – CREATING A BETTER WORLD

Being Special 177
Words 181
Hit 182
Angel 184
How To Stop A Giant 187
Letting Me Be 188

Chapter 15 – SOMETHING BEAUTIFUL TO SHARE

What's Love 191
Life's Bliss 194
Prayer 195
Gone Today Tomorrow 197
And 198

Acknowledgements 199
About The Author 201

Chapter 1
About Life

Secret

There is a secret
in life.
There is a magic
to thrive.

There is a wave
you can't see,
a mighty path
to simply Be.

There is a mountain of love
and a river of passion –
neither of these
go along with fashion.

The secret lies
between the waves,
where the yearning
for money and riches fades;

a place where
love and kindness
still reside;

a place where
greed
is left outside;

a place where
simplicity exists;

a place where
we're allowed
to resist;

a place where
good and better
don't matter, and
where souls are free to fly;

a place where
selfish thoughts dissolve
and every soul
can reach the sky;

a place where
we can give
'a piece of love'
and receive back
the other half;

a place where
love weighs
more than money
and kindness
is the career to run;

a place where
no one is left hungry
and every soul
can 'share the bun;'

a place beyond
our selfish living,
beyond the goal
to rule the world;

beyond the person's
selfish takings,
beyond respect-less
words and hurt.

The secret is,
the place is there –
it is around us,
everywhere.

Just listening
to the waves' splutter
can make us free
from
selfish clutter.

As for the waves
and the ocean,
human thoughts
have no motion.

Rain

After every raindrop
comes the sun.
Every step
is an important one.

Every smile
can change the day.
Every help
can change the way.

Every hand
can help to build.
Every gentle word
can ease the guilt.

Every decision
can change a life around.
Every care given
can reduce a 'mount.'

Think about it;
this world is shared.
So, whatever you do,
make sure it's 'cared.'

Silence Within

Where we belong,
the silent mind
makes us
strong.

Life's storms
have passed;
nothing
does
last.

Life's thunder
and hail
may
make us
frail.

It's always there, though –
a new place to begin …
which comes
from a true heart
and the silence within.

Precious Things

Diamonds and pearls
seem precious to us.
Fortunes and money
are our fuss.

Endless times
we spend on achieving
what greed and ego
goad us to believe in.

The days come and go;
we see our fortunes grow.
The truth is, though,
that we don't know

that the more we have,
the more we want – indeed –
forgetting
that life itself is not guaranteed;

that greed, and ego,
make us worry –
fights over money
are another story.

How does it happen
that, although we have plenty,
we argue and fight
with loved ones –
of these, too many.

The day will come –
most often too late –
where we learn
about another fate,

that diamonds and fortunes
do not matter,
that the rich heart
profoundly outweighs the latter.

Morning Sun

Walking
in the morning sun.
I'm late for work;
I've got to run.

Listening
to the sound of birds.
Going to work,
it deeply hurts.

Peace and calmness,
just a light wind moving the trees.
Preparing the children's lunches;
I'm already on my knees.

Peaceful sunlight
reaching through the bush.
My husband's upset
from the rush and push.

A morning's walk
among peaceful autumn leaves.
The day keeps unfolding
with more work up my sleeves.

Watching the mist
on the morning lawn.
*I'm tired of hearing
my husband's moan.*

Noticing
that nature is at ease.
*Wondering,
why so many friends
have a disease.*

Seeing the leaves
softly flying in the wind's blow.
*On my mind is the fact that
I too have to go.*

The sun stretches
over the beautiful land.
*I rush into the car,
breakfast in hand.*

How peaceful
to see nature thrive.
*I'm totally stressed,
full of strife.*

Life is full of beauty,
peace, and calm.
*How, then, do our lives
cause so much harm?*

CHAPTER 2

Overcoming Challenges

Days

Death is heaven;
life is hell.
Is this now
a common spell?

Day in, day out,
we scream aloud:
*'Life's too busy;
there's no way out!'*

Endless competition
and feeling left out,
not noticing
what our life is about.

Frustration
and pain
too often
let the belly gain.

Creating
disease,
where we want only
to be *at* ease.

Numbing the fears
with alcohol,
smoke, and chips,
until the next disaster hits.

Why can't we get the message
into our brain,
that our greed, ego, and overfeeding
don't ease the pain?

That we're the creators
of our pain and disease,
not able to change
as it's easier to please?

We keep moving along
society's bumpy road, as we grow,
because it's too easy
to just follow the flow.

No one told us:
Follow that way too much,
and the road leads to hell –
disease and such.

When we look back,
what will we see?
Life's puppet –
or the real me?

Keys

What difference
does it make,
having an important meeting –
even that piece of cake?

Everything
we do in life
has a consequence;
we hope to thrive.

We follow
the rules and our trail,
hoping for life
to be an easy sail.

How often, though,
is the way we go
our path,
or just other people's flow?

Swimming alone
we may meet a torment,
but sometimes
it's worth facing the current.

What life teaches
is 'let it be' …
but the well-trodden path
is not always the key.

Miles

How many miles
do we drive in a day,
a week, a year –
are we driving our lives away?

We swapped our legs
for the driver's seat.
We are proud of our cars
– or is it just greed?

With the legs not moving,
the body gets stiff.
We pray to get better,
only, if ….

We'd rather take pills
than get out of the car;
our doom in the future
as our health won't reach far.

With pain and diseases
plentiful looming,
all these for us,
from lack of moving.

While, back in time,
we walked many miles,
these days we sit –
stuffing our bodies with food piles.

Too much,
and too many moments each day,
we sit and waste hours
of our time away.

Imagine
(it sounds too good to be true),
but there is a way
out of the blue.

To see the future
turn bright and shine,
walk back to the old days –
before the car's time.

Buzz

A buzzing world
doesn't let us rest.
Innovations
appear to be this world's pest.

Charged up
from constant sound,
ears buzz;
heads spin around.

Ultimate electricity
running our life,
fostering the lie that
it makes us thrive?

Peace and calmness
are disappearing,
in a world charged up
from endless engineering.

Our world radiated
into a constant buzz,
devastation,
but too few raise a fuss.

Sleepless nights
from constant chatter,
all because
we don't seem to care
about the matter?

Microwaved
from the moment we get up,
we even sleep with it
and continue to fry our gut.

An electric world –
a wireless life,
cuts through our bodies
like an invisible knife.

Common diseases
crippling people we met,
hammering noises
in our head.

Love it or not
but the endless innovation zoom
may not be
this century's gloom.

A social world
though not real –
creepy,
and leaving people in constant fear.

Captured by today's disease
which we call life –
is this the ultimate challenge
(as too many don't survive)?

That's what we want?
It's what we get.
The buzz sucking up life –
don't we regret?

Be smart, find a way,
and find it soon.
Find and share
safe space and room.

Naïve

We thought
it's fun,
never assumed
the hidden gun.

A life
of riches;
would never have believed
the ditches.

The social world,
a gift for us,
all online, eerie –
but we don't make a fuss.

A world of data
we supply, every day,
to an enemy
searching for its prey.

We share our life
with the virtual world,
never thinking
that we might get hurt;

that our careless sharing
may disrupt the world
in a way
never before heard.

We give away
our secrets and thoughts,
triggering enemies' weapons
we never fought.

A weapon,
secretly catching our brain,
making us vulnerable
and creating pain?

A weapon,
changing the world as it is,
as it plays our emotions and scares …
So it is.

We invite the giant
to 'manipulate me,'
with the dream, lost,
of being free.

A herd nature
created with this,
like sheep and cattle;
what bliss.

A giant idea that
– with simply a hiss –
makes us act like animals
in their circus?

We are tracked and traced
in our homes and cars.
We give permission,
not imagining the looming scars.

A social world
we love to share,
that's how we feed
the world's biggest scare.

One day we may wake up
from the fake scene.
On time?
Or as a slave
to the 'virtual' dream?

Watching The Wind

Watching the wind
makes me think.
Does it not matter
if my species goes extinct?

A daily battle
for species like me,
all gone
or declined in numbers.
Is that the future we'll see?

Insects destroyed
by pest control;
flowers gone,
replaced by
a concrete wall.

Bees are disappearing,
the new world doesn't comply.
Birds die, even young ones,
where there's no food supply.

Pest control used
for cheap food we buy
or for lawn and garden
to look pretty –
no matter if insects die.

Native land stripped
for paper and wood.
Oceans heated,
which does us no good.

Too many cats are roaming
and killing native birds.
Humans appear not to care
how all this hurts.

Animals dying
from rubbish thrown out.
If you were the dying animal
you *would* care,
no doubt.

We need a new law
to protect our world.
There must be an end
to the senseless hurt,

a law for all species
and the killing en masse.
Humans beware;
it's not such a fuss.

We can all do our bit
to make things better.
Otherwise,
there may be no future
for the latter.

You don't care
about the thoughts of the winds?
You'll see
what the future brings.

A concrete world
with no birds to be heard?
Stale and dead oceans,
a choking world.

Life on Earth
gone as we know?
It's our choice;
we can still give it a go.

Chapter 3

Making Life Easy

Happiness Goal

Down and dusted,
that's how we feel?
Dreams shattered,
looking for a magic heal?

Whatever way,
it seems to be,
a change of direction
and a change of appeal.

It's easy to wait
for help to come.
A better outcome,
though, is our own run.

There never was
a magic fly
that could fly through the glass
into the sky.

The way to go
is the way to move –
away from our misery,
finding a way to improve.

Away from business,
away from fortunes and money,
there is a secret magic,
like honey.

What counts in life is
finding the smooth way.
It's finding our own way
that makes the day.

Nature
is the secret of life.
Let nature make you
live and thrive.

Be mindful
of the world going round;
its cycle can turn
any misery around.

Move your body,
move your soul –
this is the way
to your happiness goal!

Life Is

For some,
life is heaven, but
for some
it's a spell.

Some
have it all,
while some
may never do well.

For what reason
we'll never know,
but we can learn
while on the go.

One thing we know
is, no matter what,
we're never the only ones
who get kicked in the gut.

No matter what pain
or what we mourn,
the pain we go through
is all well known.

Through life we learn
much pain, much regret –
some would never have thought of
how hard it can get.

No matter what pain,
there is a key.
Letting pain rule our life
makes no one free.

What happens in life
is for a reason.
We need to accept
what we can't change
and learn self-pleas'n ...

Let's face it –
making our life hard
helps no one,
not even our own heart.

The key is
to love life as it is
and to cherish
memories and bliss.

Moving on
from pains that matter
to a life
that makes us better.

There is no help
for anyone
with years of mourning
to be done.

Friend,
I know how it feels,
but sadness and suffering
don't help,
nor do they support our appeals.

Life is to be lived,
lived even through the blue
no matter what –
that is the clue.

Forget about
the *pity* and the *grim*
and set yourself up
for a WIN!

The truth is, we are not born
into this world's history
to make our life
a misery.

One Of Them

It is fearful,
often depressing ...
They look strong
and appear impressing.

They look as good
as it gets.
To our mind,
they win the bets.

They are
calm; they are fearless.
They leave us
feeling an incredible mess.

They seem to be
high above.
Secretly, though,
we're *all* doing it tough.

It is the way of the world.
It seems
that everyone else
has better themes.

The truth is,
not only what *we* see is real.
It's *all* of us; we all
experience that daunting feel.

All we need
is belief in ourselves;
then we'll know
the feeling of wealth.

Stuff Up

Bet I stuffed it up
again.
Got myself
once more in a jam.

Feels like
it's what I do best,
though it hurts
the stomach and chest.

Feeling guilty?
What's the point?
What's welded
is already joined.

The fact is,
we can't change the past,
but we can learn from it
at last.

Trust

Do we know what
trust is all about?
Who can be trusted?
Say it. Aloud.

We trust the family,
neighbours, and friends.
We trust tenants
to pay their rents.

Honestly –
do you think
what people say is true? Or
do you believe in stories
that come out of the blue?

Too many people
fully agree
that our family
can become
our biggest enemy.

What is it
that many friends care about:
to live in wealth,
selfish and loud?

We trust the world
that *we* don't get harmed …
but we know
that animals get hurt
when they're greedily farmed.

If everyone
had peace in mind,
why is there so much harm
to the world
and humankind?

It's not just
the wars and disease;
it's too often
our human nature
that destroys the peace.

You wonder
what this has to do …
Face it!
The only one
you can truly trust
is *you*.

What's Special About Me

What's special
about me
is a secret, and
always will be.

For if you knew
all about me –
it would take any special-ness
away from me!

If there is anything special
about any *'me,'*
it's best to be simply fulfilled;
won't you agree?

CHAPTER 4

Health And Know-How

Every Day Is A Feast

Every day is a feast;
gourmet is the value.
We fancy the finest for our moods.

Not thinking ahead,
it's today's pleasure we desire.
We wallow in luxury and exquisite foods.

No physical exertion is required
for pleasing feeds,
as the shelves effortlessly supply
all our needs.

While most of our life
we spend in the seat,
in endless feasts
of pleasure and greed,

there comes the day
when being rich doesn't matter,
when, for the body,
fortunes don't make it better.

While we worry about
being injured or harmed,
for daily excesses
the body's not armed.

We worry for the kids growing up safe
and not being deceived.
What does it matter,
with the parents deceased?

We take flowers
to people we know,
knowing it's due to the cancer
that does wildly grow.

We meet them disabled,
or ill in their home,
not thinking that much suffering
comes from food alone.

What do we know about
evolution and riches?
Today's feasts
don't cover the bridges.

Is this the time
where it all turns around?
Where taking too much
sends our world to the ground?

Where we are
taking life for granted –
captured by lavishness,
and enchanted?

We love to indulge –
but with blinkers set.
Every day is a feast,
but – what do we get?

Oh Boy!

Oh boy,
What have they done to us?
Feeding
with processed foods en masse.

Sure,
don't we enjoy the taste?
Plenty of oil, salt, and sugar,
no waste?

Enjoying
processed foods aplenty,
unfortunately
makes the body cranky.

There is
no place on the label
that tells the truth
about our food on the table.

That many years in,
we may regret
today's food choices.
You bet.

For many of us
it may come too late,
with the body
already suffering its sad fate.

With pains aplenty
and immobility,
in need of help to
just go for a pee?

Too late then
for the fight;
why don't we try now
to make it right?

Who do you think
will care for you
if senseless consumption
is the contributing clue?

The smart way is
to change it now.
Leave processed foods on shelves,
and foster a happy cow.

Betrayed

Health is
what we're looking for,
but the system
makes us sore.

There is much pain
we are going through,
with plenty of diseases
for me and you.

'Just go
and take another pill.'
They don't tell us that
the pills may kill.

Years go by
with our bodies diseased,
and much weight we gain ...
we don't get told
that our diet and lifestyle
are to blame.

The food we eat is well in profit
and big business's hand.
Is that the reason
we stick our heads in the sand?

Plenty of chicken
is healthy – that's what we believe,
when it's known to destroy our joints
and cause other diseases for us to grieve.

Plenty of milk
is supposed to be good for bone health,
though it's known to feed cancer
and destroy our bones' tissue and wealth.

Plenty of meat
is said to be needed by us,
tough the truth is
this wrecks arteries and guts.

Reality teaches the result
from being overfed,
with years of disease
and plenty of regret.

Diseases
that destroy the fun,
in the long months and years
after the indulge has begun.

You really want to destroy
your body, allowing your cancer to grow?
Keep feeding it
plenty of milk, meat, sugar, and alcohol.

What do you think,
my fellow human?
Instead of stuffing ourselves
we'd better get movin'!

If there is a way
to health and happiness,
why don't we make it
the story of our success?

Looking Beyond

'Vegan'
is a scary word;
for many people
it seems to hurt.

It's for 'hippies'
and 'crazy ones' –
not for ourselves,
good daughters and sons.

The myth is big,
the stories unreal –
but how
does it really feel?

Living vegan
is not just a word,
it's about making sure
no being gets hurt.

Living in a kind world,
cruelty-free,
that is
a true vegan philosophy.

Living in a world
without cruelty,
where kindness
to all humans and creatures
is reality.

Living in a world
being kind to ourselves,
as food from animals
creates disease
and harms our body cells.

Living in a world
with a perfect 'expect',
a healthy body
and no regret.

Living a happy
and healthy life,
without harming other creatures,
whether dead or alive.

Living beautiful,
as most people don't know
that nature's supply
is a real beauty's way to go.

Vegan is being smart
in every matter,
knowing that hurting animals
doesn't make things better.

Instead of closing
our eyes to the world,
vegans can see
where all get hurt.

Here it is,
all you need to know as a whole.
Vegan is being kind to the world,
your own body, and your soul.

Never Too Late

Old and stiff
it feels.
Can't even touch
my heels.

Life's taken its toll,
we believe,
like being captured
by a relentless thief;

taking out
our energy and strength,
our ability
and movement length?

The truth is,
there's no such thing,
just like the myth of
struggling to stay slim.

It's up to us
and our mind,
to keep on moving,
leaving the stiffness behind.

As good
as it gets,
these are
the bets.

Life's
trusting you
to get
the clue.

There is only one way
to get fit,
and this applies
through all ages hit.

The fact is,
stiffness is not our fate.
Start moving now –
it's never too late.

Growing Old

What a laugh and what a pity
we may feel for the old,
only until
we too grow wrinkled and bald.

Feeling sorry
for the old?
It's not the care of
the young and the bold.

Though, as we grow
and the older we become,
we soon find
there's a pattern in life to run.

What we watch
in others today,
we'll all experience ourselves
along the way.

No matter
how absurd to hold,
remember – every generation
is growing old.

A smart move is
to cherish the old,
and learn from the lessons
they have been told.

A lesson to learn here is:
don't be nuts –
take care of your
mind, body, and guts.

Too many people
fall into the indulgence trap
with old age, pain,
and plenty of regret.

Keeping life healthy and young
is the key; be smart.
Look after your body
for health, long life, and vitality.

Chapter 5
A World Around Us

Happiness Is ...

Give your hand to a stranger;
see the beauty around.
Be one with nature
and feel the world go round.

See the person
in need –
even help
a lost sheep.

Happiness is
what we care about;
what we can give
with love and no doubt.

Happiness is
to receive vitality
from someone
who loves the same strategy.

Happiness
can be everywhere.
All we need is
to share and care.

Gone Shopping

We are on the move,
but where do we go?
Finding the truth
that disappeared long ago?

Nothing matters
but daily routines.
'Keep on going'
if you know what it means.

What seems to be today's drive
is shopping for bits,
all just to please
the neighbours, friends, and kids.

Emotionless,
we follow our daily tasks,
unaware
that pretending is just another mask.

Tired
and stressed,
and
unable to rest.

We work, we shop,
and we wander headless,
going in circles,
too often reckless.

What do we see
when we look around?
Motionless faces
that are lost and unbound?

The confused spirits
of life's merry-go-round
and the true souls
gone, to never be found.

Façade

Who
are we?
And
what will be?

It's not
just the make-up;
it's a façade of life
that we've built up.

Just like the make-up
that covers our faces,
the façade
doesn't leave room for spaces.

A fake world it is
that we live in.
True feelings and honesty
are giving in.

To keep the façade,
loved ones may crawl on their knees;
instead of respecting their need,
we require them to please.

Nothing matters.
We've got to fit in,
desperately trying
to match the fake world we live in.

Although it creates
despair and turmoil,
we keep running the track
we pretend to enjoy.

What is important
about the clothes we wear?
What we say in public
and for what we care?

Why don't we notice
that, too often, and too much,
we live a lie
and keep grasping a crutch?

What we do
is betray ourselves and our health,
trying to live in a world
not real, with fake wealth.

The real world
is an honest one, and kind,
with no hurt and harm
to find;

a wonderful place
where we don't need
to compare with friends,
family, and greed;

where love rules,
and gentle care,
instead of constant competition,
pain, and despair.

A heaven
that we dream about
is in our hands –
it just needs to be lived out.

Chaos

What about a person who
doesn't fit in?
A too-sincere and kind being
from within?

Neither an adult,
nor a kid?
Left in the middle
and … doesn't fit?

Not belonging,
but heartily longing?
Not captured at all
but truly loyal?

Not expected
and too often rejected?
Influential and
strangely deferential?

Not a child in mind
but mysteriously kind?
Not accepted
but disrespected?

Not fearful
but hurt and tearful?
A kind soul shattered, from hurt and harm
by human acts and firearm?

There is something in life
we never learn.
There's no need to fight
for the norm for which we yearn.

One Wonders

Kindness is dying,
respect disappearing.
It's a lost game –
why are we still cheering?

What is it
that we care about?
Is it just money and riches
that make us proud?

Forgotten
seem the simple things,
and no one wonders
what this brings.

Gold Rush

A better world
it seems to be.
We have it all,
but we won't be free.

Luxurious houses,
yachts, and mansions,
we show it all off yet
still worry about pensions.

Time flies by;
we work long hours to pay the bills –
plenty of those
for doctors, alcohol, drugs, and pills!

The fact is that the richer we become,
the more we pile on in
weight, drugs, and pills –
with disease yet to come.

God bless the *'poor'*, as they are the richest
in a golden heart and a joyful mind.
Teachers they are to us
for true wealth of another kind,

reminding us
that the truth in life
is far beyond
what we can buy
with money, fortunes,
and bond.

The truth is
that souls are alive,
and we don't need
fortunes to thrive.

If we keep thinking
it's money and fortunes that count,
we will truly miss,
for it's not the money
but our inner peace, happiness, and bliss.

Here

Heartburn …
Yearn.

A difference to feel?
Heal?

What fear?
The future is here.

CHAPTER 6

Lessons To Learn

Thank You, Mum

What have you been through
over many years, and *'back then'*?
Now a tiny virus
seems to start it all again.

War and Depression,
no food on the plate,
why once more for you?
Is it fate?

You've been working and fighting
through all those years.
What you have done for me
puts me to tears.

Mum, you are my hero,
my biggest one.
You always cared, though – often –
it would have been easier
just to run.

Mum, you never left;
you were never gone
despite all the hardship –
which almost won.

Mum, thanks to you
this world has me.
A world, and all its beauty, that –
thanks to you – I can see.

Mum, you always
showed me the sun,
no matter how far
I wanted to run.

Mum, you taught me lessons
from the many years of pain,
that there is struggle in life
but always an end to the rain;

that no matter
how hard life may become,
there will always be
another day of sun.

Mum, you are always
there for me.
I pray for you
to be happy and healthy.

Be sure:
You will always be
with me.

Matters

Life
is all about 'me,'
but what would we pay
to have our minds free?

We whinge
and complain,
searching
for others to blame.

Do we ever
accept?
Life is never
going to be perfect.

Instead of learning
and finding a solution,
we stick to fast tracking
and further confusion.

Our mind makes sure
to keep us on track,
predominantly
for our ego's 'feedback.'

Instead of letting go
and creating peace,
the ego's rule
gives everyone griefs.

Imagine
how easy life could be
if it wasn't
all about 'me'?

We want the best
for us and the kids,
and we are always right –
no matter how the truth fits.

We feel superior
in our race.
What if we were born
in a different colour, in this case?

Our minds are occupied
with money and things,
with what people say,
and what the future brings.

Think about it,
I'm asking you.
There is a rule in life,
and this holds true.

We dwell in the past
and plan our way
but we miss out enjoying
the moment and day.

Invasion

The dark times
began many years ago,
but still
there is nowhere to go.

Dying en masse
are the creatures of this Earth,
in prisons and tortured
for the invaders' selfish worth.

The world we live in
destroyed, strip by strip,
in too many places
Earth appears a big tip.

Recklessly taking
what nature did create,
not caring a bit
about the Earth's fate.

It is a war
against all in existence,
not stopping at cruelty
nor any resistance.

The Earth, as it is, seems
doomed to die.
This knowledge still
doesn't make invaders shy.

Invaders have taken
the lead here with greed;
they keep taking it all,
focused on their own species' breed.

Although it's already too much
For Earth to cope,
invaders keep breeding,
not heeding a note.

Dark ... dangerous ... cruel,
too frightening to face,
Earth's creatures are hiding,
are fenced in or kept in caged place.

The invader, though, keeps doing
what only suits him,
and whatever is wasted
just goes 'in the bin.'

You may wonder,
'What is all this fuss?'
Human – think!
The *Dark Invader* on Earth is – us!

Lost Season

Heaven knows,
what a disgrace;
the loving season
has turned into a race.

Where once tender loving
and kindness was the device,
it's now about cars,
presents, and price.

Endless gifts
to be carried around;
the true Christmas spirit
nowhere to be found.

Where once children's eyes
lit up with simple joys,
kids today are stressed out
from choosing too many toys.

Where once we were treated
with an orange and nuts,
we feast today
and grow obese butts.

Silent tinsels
are reminding us
of a better time,
without all the fuss.

A time where Christmas
was not just simple and kind
but a time to rest
for the human mind.

What have we done
to the Christmas spirit,
that it disappeared?
We can't even hear it.

All we are left with
is stress, feasts, and bills;
many of us are
only coping with pills.

Why don't we start
listening to our heart?
It's where the true spirit lives
which is torn apart.

Burned

The Earth is burning,
but conscience icy-cold?
Do politics matter?
Beware what the future will hold.

Rivers dry;
decisions are made.
Fish floating in death
where all hopes fade.

Egos and money matter –
who's got a clue?
So it is, the future
in the hands of a few?

Will you beat the great and care?
Saving our nations from despair?
Temptations – easily met.
Beware the thoughts of future regret.

This world is shared,
don't you agree?
It's not all about fortunes
and the 'me.'

Is the devil behind
today's turning wheels?
Just to be pleased,
must we follow its heels?

It's too easy to follow
the given trail,
even though
it makes us frail?

A slave to
what our world has become,
like rats on a boat
round the 'circus' we run?

Awareness is
what's stopping the rat
from going down
the deadly trap.

We want life
to be free, and to last.
Make sure it's the future –
not just our past.

Trojan

The world
at war.
In some 100 years,
they'll wonder
about the roar.

An enemy
makes the world freeze in fear;
a disease
turns nightmares into real.

The weapons
are toilet paper and tish –
are we going back to the old times
where newspapers were feeding the fish?

An alien monster,
too tiny to see,
brings the entire world
to its knee?

Run away
in the car or a boat?
Make sure you take the toilet paper
and cat litter load.

No one gets off
the last cruise trip,
while the world around
is having a fit.

Get on a plane
with your pack?
Bad idea;
you might never get back.

A war
like none have ever seen before,
the world in lockdown …
and there is more.

Everyone's a prisoner
as we get hurt.
No hugs, no kisses –
is that the new
scary world?

The evil is here
and it strikes us all.
A tiny virus?
What a flaw.

Unsmart

It's on again,
giving
everyone pain.

Souls
are lost
at unbearable
cost.

For what
does a human body count?
Is it nothing,
just to be buried in the ground?

What is it
we are fighting for?
Does it really matter?
Or,

is it just our selfish pride,
greed, and joy,
perhaps
to test a new war toy?

Is it
our selfish rule
or
just acting the fool?

Endless suffering
in the name of pride?
For decent people
no place to hide?

Think about it;
how would it be
if we were born
on the other side?
Would we still agree?

What is the fighting
all about
if in the end
it just creates doubt?

There is a truth
about fighting and wars:
no one wins;
it just creates sores.

But even now,
as for thousands of years,
the smart way –
of freedom and peace –
just disappears.

Chapter 7

If We'd Only Listen

Voices

Don't we hear them,
loud and clear?
At any life's crossing
they will appear.

Voices are showing us
the way to go –
but we know better,
picking our own,
and setting off with the flow.

Voices,
the angels of our time,
are guiding the way,
though,
mostly, we decline.

'I should have …'
is what we say at last,
but the voice … we continue to ignore it,
just like in the past.

Watch Out

You've got to
watch out –
danger is everywhere,
round and about.

We may get eaten by sharks
(once in a while),
bitten by snakes,
or perhaps a crocodile.

There are accidents –
too many of them,
domestic violence –
too much, again.

We may
get hit by a car
or we may
get shot from afar.

But
what we don't think about,
though
it should be screamed out loud!

Is that, although we're not
raised in a pouch,
most of us die
from sitting on the couch.

Silence

Silence,
joy.
No,
it's not a toy.

It's not
to buy;
it does not come
from having pie.

It's not from
material or matter,
but it does make
everyone's life better.

It's not
for sale.
It's
very frail.

It's a shine
from the heart.
It's part of nature's
work of art.

It's within
people's chatter
as nothing other
will matter.

It's not
what you gain,
but it comes
with the rain.

It doesn't
take space,
but it will stop
the race,

as it's not
what we win,
but it comes
from within.

Stop

Stop
looking at the clock.
Time
is not life's major crop.

Time
is more a crucial block
as ageing seems
our inner clock.

Stop wasting life
worrying about time.
Time is not
our reason for decline.

The time we have
is time to be,
in the present,
and feel the 'me.'

For in the present
time does stop;
love resides
and nature's crop.

Nothing matters
in the 'now.'
Time is only
for the world to show.

Time *is*;
we cannot change the game,
but we can change
the time to blame.

Stop the run
and look around.
Watch the moment;
it's profound.

Stop
and
watch
life's
true magic …

As our constant run
through life,
is simply
tragic.

Lost

Lost for good?
Like a mask it feels.
Faces dead,
like motionless wheels.

Where is it gone?
Will it come back?
Look around;
it's lost on the track.

Waxed faces
with no motion observed.
Habits?
Or just disbursed?

Sometimes it tries to sneak back on track,
cheery and hopeful,
though
strange looks we get back.

Hope is not lost;
it's still around.
A gentle smile
can still be our common ground.

Sunrise

Sunrise –
since the darkest time,
don't expect life
to be 'just fine.'

What it is
to believe,
is for us
to achieve.

CHAPTER 8

Love And Other Dilemmas

Love

Is it really
what we think;
love is heaven –
or a boat that'll sink?

We are famous
for belief that
marriage is
our relief.

No, pal; true love
is up to you
to make it right,
or turn it all to goo.

It is your input
that's the matter.
If you're not prepared,
forget about the latter.

Love is giving
and caring for one.
Love is respecting and cherishing
the other one.

Love is being
in the moment with one,
forgetting time and desire
for the world to run.

Love is sharing
a dreadful day,
making it better
for both that way.

Love is to know
what you desired and wanted,
sharing your own need
but not expecting anything granted.

Love is appreciating
every happy day.
Love is dealing with the bad ones
in another way.

Love is sharing,
no matter what,
being honest and grateful
for anything but.

Love is being you
with the other,
loving yourself as much as
loving your sister and brother;

knowing that only
when you love yourself,
you can be kind
to another self.

The story is simple.
It's what we believe,
that is for us
to achieve.

Cry

Time
goes by.
Why do we need
to cry?

Missing
the lost?
How much
does it cost?

Tears
for those gone,
often
too strong.

Why do we cry *for* the dead
when they are gone,
if we can cry *with* them
while we belong?

Isn't life's
running by
the real reason
to cry?

Time
is the game,
with daily business
and life's challenges to blame.

All I want is to
be with 'you.'
Suddenly, you're gone –
with no time to tell what's true.

What's the point
of mourning the dead,
when we can choose
to be mindful together in life
instead?

Life's too often shortened,
no matter how old,
where life's challenges
cancel life's hold.

Are we truly
not aware
that its daily routines
we could better share?

What is
any fighting for
if we end up mourning,
or …?

Why fighting
over *'anything but'*
if we miss out
on a kiss, or a hug?

What's the use
of mourning the dead
if we can kiss and hug
in life instead?

Love You All

Under one roof,
is it hubby to blame?
Is it the kids
who send me insane?

Today it's the dishes,
tomorrow the bin.
It's crazy –
why can't we win?

Can't stand
the many questions you ask.
Honey, I love you,
but I'm not up to the task.

The kids drive me mad,
now calls your dad.
Just talked to my mum –
why am *I* the one that's the 'family fun'?

Need some room.
Need some space.
Honey, let go –
we're not in a race.

Need a bath.
Need soaking in.
Here come the kids –
Love you, but please – not again!

One day of work,
that's it for me.
Grandma, love you and your cake,
but not today's tea.

Weekend now.
Pleasure time.
Instead, it's the family over
for barbie and wine.

Please let me go;
let me rest –
a peaceful Mother's Day
at best?

Love you all,
and love the fun,
but need a rest
from the constant run.

Cherish

Time goes fast
day by day.
Aren't we always
'on our way?'

Isn't there constantly
something to do?
With our life passing by,
we don't have a clue.

The day may come
when we all regret,
that we have wasted precious times,
I truly bet.

Don't ever miss
cherishing a loved one;
your mother, father,
daughter, or son.

Stop letting
the little troubles creep in,
the fights
and blaming others of sin.

Cherish
every moment you crave
as you can't take them
into your grave.

Every moment,
every second, is of worth,
so share your love
with your cherished ones on Earth.

Don't wait
till it's too late,
as every day
can be that final fate.

Cherish blissful moments
and time.
Don't ever waste them
as happiness is on the line.

Truly cherish
Every moment, every sec –
make sure
there can be no regret.

Don't Miss

There is something in life
not to miss.

It's true love,
and
'life's kiss.'

Chapter 9

People We Meet

Andrea

Why
are you doing this to me?
Like you,
I just want to live and be.

A family person
you are said to be,
instead, you're making sure
other families crawl on their knee.

Do you have chats
with friends at work?
Of your cruelty
they most likely never heard.

You dress in smart clothes
and 'show off' at the office
while driving sincere people
over the abyss.

What do you get from
being that nasty 'you'?
I bet your family
does not have a clue.

How can you do
to other ones
what you would never want
to experience just once.

If you or your kids
were treated your way,
you'd be in tears
and make people pay.

Andrea,
what you have done to this world
is of no words
but was, luckily, heard.

There is a lesson
from what you have done.
Cruelty
has never won.

Therefore beware
if you're the nasty one;
the truth is always there, and
out it will come.

Life's Pity

What a pity,
life itself?
No, it's fellow humans
who commonly wreck our self.

No, it's not just killings
and fights in the bar,
it's every day's business
that doesn't get us far.

The rules we obey,
and we have to be strict
even though others suffer –
that we can predict.

This world has lost
the caring sense.
It's rules and business
we enhance.

Can't we look
behind the scene?
Where happiness
for all is keen?

Rules and business
don't belong
where simpler ways
get us far beyond.

It's an old truth
we have forgotten
which is the line
at the very bottom.

*'What's the point
of sticking to the road of rules
if potholes on the way
break our shoes?'*

Ladders

What a pleasure
to be rich;
to have it all
appears to be life's pitch.

Up the ladder
with blinkers on –
not looking down,
away, or beyond.

Rich thick soles
stop the pain
from crushing others
on the way to gain.

Where greed resides
there is no space
for compassion, love,
or life's true grace.

We may be rich
and have reached the goal,
but on the way
we have lost our soul.

Let Go

They are
fierce,
don't heed
a word;

desire
to win,
with
the wicked grin.

They please themselves
and don't care.
They won't see another person's need,
nor a reason to share.

Please yourself;
climb up the ladder.
Who doesn't suit,
thrown aside like bad spatter.

Be careful, friend,
as all you will win
is the scary grin
within.

Being Social

Icy cold air,
an icy cold wave,
'It's warmer here,'
sounds from the grave.

Too many souls
live in despair
from fellow humans
who don't care.

What is supposed to be
a social thrill,
too often turns ugly
and threatens to kill.

The smart ones know,
more than the other,
that the bullied ones
are not to suffer.

But the ones
who play the ugly part,
live in hell throughout life
and beyond life depart.

Loving You

We are your family
but also your deepest fear.
'It's all to help',
that's what you hear.

All we do is for your happiness.
It doesn't matter
if you get crushed along the way,
we guess.

Making life happy
for you,
that's apparently what families
have to do.

We think
for you,
but that
takes life from you.

We want to be
with you, not realising
that way
we stifle you.

We are upset
when you say
you don't appreciate our loving,
'debilitating' way.

Seemingly
we do it all for your good,
but how dare you
decline our ego's food!

It's all for *you,*
that's what we say.
– No, lovey,
it's for the ego's way!

The fact is,
what we think is good
might be suffocating others
despite sharing the same root.

The smart way is
to forget the bond
and see the truth;
look beyond.

Start seeing life
as reality.
Take on life –
but set your family free.

Chapter 10
Doom, Gloom, And Politics

Right Or Wrong

Belief
is strong.
Trust,
all gone?

A world
in turmoil,
on many countries'
home soil.

Thoughts thrown around
in vast amount,
onto us,
shaking safe ground.

Although unreal,
who is to say?
And who
is on the right way?

Beliefs suspicious?
History redrawn?
Thoughts scary.
Humanity gone?

There is one certain truth
left in this world:
we must make sure
no one gets hurt.

While we can be sorry for
being wrong,
there is no saying sorry
for hurting others
while we feel strong.

No matter
what's right or wrong,
we've *got* to care for each other.
Otherwise, we may not be
just wrong,
but we'll lose our souls on the way along.

Cooking The Chef

Our precious world
is getting hot.
We are cooking ourselves –
a dangerous stock.

Ingredients
are not just a few
and are all adding up
to the toxic stew.

Plenty of fuel
and toxic trash,
from airplanes, boats, and cars –
all feeding this world's crash.

Have you
ever thought about
our meat consumption's
toxic methane pour out?

That our deodorants
and other sprays
destroy the world
in other ways?

And do we care
about our litter?
Why is our rubbish so much?
It's turning the world bitter.

What doesn't suit
goes in the bin –
who cares that
nature is growing thin?

We litter the bush,
the streets, and the ocean.
We even use toxic oils
in our skin lotion.

We are growing
a cocktail of toxic mix.
How do we think
we can find a fix?

The boiling heat
our air cons push into the air
only add further
to the despair.

Everyone, go on
and spoil the Earth,
for it appears we deem
our children's unworth.

Human,
hàve you got a thought to spare?
Or is that all you can do,
pollute land and air?

Using up nature's treasures,
burning coal and stealing its gas?
On top of all those we use, the atom's
yet another deadly class.

What on Earth
allows us to blame
everyone else
for the 'shame'?

We need to see
that it's each one of us
who gives the stew
a toxic buzz.

If we all continue
to need our 'kick,'
we're all to blame
for our world being sick.

No, Minister

Did you get it
wrong?
Or are you speaking
with a forked tongue?

The message you get,
do you listen to it?
Doesn't it tell you
that the world is going to 'fit'?

There is a voice
inside all – including you –
that is always telling us
what's true.

Harming others,
is that the way?
Ruining the climate?
'This can't be,' does it say?

If you listen to
what's deep inside,
there is only love and compassion
for this world's ride.

Compassion
for all human being,
for our kids' future
and the world's wellbeing.

Look what ignorance
has done:
wars, floods, and fires –
even now too much to overcome.

Devastation in the rivers;
no insects,
there won't be butterflies
without caterpillars.

It's easy to destroy
the world we live in,
although the ego
may give it the grin.

Trust your inner voice;
make things right.
Egos are only here
for picking a fight.

You might see the money
and good life begin,
but listening to the ego
will only destroy;
it's a sin.

No, Minister, please –
don't go wrong;
only listening to your heart
will make you strong.

Change

Changing fast,
change is free?
We are on the ride,
all of us – you and me.

Do we care
what the future brings?
Who will forgive
our daily sins?

The world is changing;
we are getting hot.
Do we know the end
to the climate's plot?

There are the ones
who do not care.
Well, life in general
doesn't seem to be fair.

Oceans poisoned,
creatures die …
a destroyed world left behind
for our kids to cry?

No, we're strong;
we raise our voice.
We opt for the chance;
we have a choice.

The challenge, though,
can you see?
For setting the world
and climate free?

The change here
is for us to 'be.'
It's up to us,
won't you agree?

We demand
big business to change,
but are we prepared
to change what's within *our* range?

What's heating the world
is the car we drive,
plane flights, and the holiday cruise
just for a dive.

Who wants to give up
eating plenty of meat?
Although it's well known
to be a major
climate cheat.

We use much energy
and endless modern devices;
things are not fancy
if we don't have the nicest.

We want a healthy
world for our kids
but spoil them with anything,
no matter how it fits.

Perhaps it's the challenge
we face this day.
We've got to change *ourselves*,
or our world slips away.

Bad Luck

Supposed to be a human being,
the new soul slipped into another world.
A devastating mistake occurred
to show how many of us are hurt.

Endless suffering for us,
in pain,
only to please
the human feast chain.

Locked up in cages
for a seemingly endless cruel life,
devastation and pain would make you prefer death
to staying alive.

A mother
has her babies stolen from her;
bashed and shattered
right in front of her.

Who would acknowledge
that daily violence and rape
is well used and accepted
to please humans and their shape?

That ice-creams and cream cakes
are only made
through suffering
and an animal's cruel fate.

Hit with sticks
and bashed along,
cruel humans make sure
there is no place to shelter from.

In daily pain
throughout their existence,
but humans don't care
about the animals' desperate resistance.

Bodily harm –
how can it be
that humans don't care
to the least degree?

That, just to please
human greed and feast,
humans create suffering
to any living thing, any beast.

The pain they go through
for humankind
can't be accepted
by any mind.

My friend, I wonder
what you would do
if the suffering creature
you're planning to eat –
was *you*?

Chapter 11

You Are Not Alone

Time Of Our Life

There comes a time
where you may find, in life,
that hurt and pain
are all part of being alive.

Terrible actions from people
may break you;
some may hurt, threaten, follow,
or intimidate you.

Just to
name only a few,
this list goes on,
with more pain for you.

Nightmares,
tremendous and daunting,
might be there
forever, haunting.

When the iceberg
tips around,
and you feel you're sinking
with it to the ground,

don't give up –
at least start crawling;
every click of the meter counts
towards your restoring.

It may be weeks
and months and years
where you struggle,
and it may come
with way too many tears.

Even though
your body is bruised,
battled, and cut,
there is always a chance
for your counter-attack.

There is a strong power
to help you pull through,
this secret weapon
that is YOU.

Alien World

The strangest feeling;
no-one's aware.
You can't explain,
but it's still there.

Tears behind
a 'beautiful' smile;
no-one sees them
in a world hostile.

The friendly smile,
the helping hand,
the love to care –
all run down in the sand.

No matter
how much you try,
in the end,
the 'daemon' kills the smile.

And no matter
how much you're longing to take part,
moments later
it's all ripped apart.

A terrified alien
in a senseless world,
seeking shelter
but never heard.

The only safe haven
that truly exists
is to stay away, alone,
and persist.

Brink

Deepest
despair,
feelings
you can't share,

empty
and hollow,
lost,
through and thorough.

The sun darkened,
the wind icy cold,
nothing left
in darkness' hold.

Wisdom is
to sit it through,
find a way
back to 'you.'

Darkness never holds;
nothing can delude.
Finding love for yourself
will always change the mood.

Of what sadness, betrayal,
and disappointment brings –
in life,
we all get a glimpse.

We can all be winners, though,
in one way,
as love, care, and compassion
will always pay.

Fate

Hell on Earth
is what you feel;
'daemons' inside
turning life 'unreal.'

Blue skies are darkened;
the sun disappears.
Living and surviving the day
become your biggest fears.

God knows from where
the deepest despair evolves
when the 'daemon' quietly
fastens its holds.

Dreams shatter
and life seems to disappear.
All that's left is emptiness,
with night and sunrise to fear.

Every step an endless effort,
every move restless and feared;
just pain to record
and sadness geared.

An endless hole
without any light,
where you fight to get out
only to fall back inside.

No one knows
the feeling within.
It's daily survival,
but hopeless and grim.

There seems one way out
that you dare to take.
They call it a sin;
it's never your fate.

The goal is
to never give in.
Believe in yourself.
In the end,
you'll win.

Here It Comes

Here it comes,
sneaking in,
feeling
like the devil's win.

It takes your will
and takes your soul,
leaving you
without a goal.

Deprived
of any living feeling,
left in emptiness
with no hope of healing.

Days go by
when hope wants to rise,
only to be shattered
into another black sunrise.

Desperation
leads the day;
hopelessness
is another way.

Paralysed
from the feeling inside,
holding your thoughts
on the scariest ride.

No motion
appears to truly help.
No effort
seems to enable self-help.

Whatever you try
seems to dissolve
in emptiness and death,
leaving the body motionless.

How to rise
from the 'devil's hold'
is the tale
we should be told.

Survival is
the way to go;
move the body
and the soul.

For as long as we keep moving,
pain will pass,
and long-yearned-for happiness
we'll gain at last.

Appreciating true love
and nature's beauty
may be the key –
and perhaps our duty.

Leave Me Alone

It's not the plan
though it's just there,
feelings inside;
no-one's aware.

With every glimpse
of a sunny day,
comes the cold dark hand
that takes it away.

The cold feeling
grabbing hold of you,
leaving only darkness and cold
to go through.

How can we turn
the dark hand away?
What can be done
to feel just ok?

It's a miracle needed
that's not in hand,
but with time passing
we'll win in the end.

Fear

Where
the ocean rolls,
where
the thunder growls,

where there is
no light in the mist,
where heavy rain
persists,

there is
no need for fear
so long as
your true soul is near.

Chapter 12

Set Up For A Win

Free

Too long
I haven't seen;
don't know
where I've been.

What's done, what happened
won't stop me
from making a change
and now breaking free.

Now is the time
to make a change,
wisdom tells,
although it feels strange.

It's time
to be me.
It's time
to be free.

I know
I too have the right
to see the sun,
shining and bright.

No matter
what holds me down,
I can make it happen –
even move to another town.

I can do it;
it's up to me –
be strong, courageous,
and break free.

If in need, I know
there is help out there.
I know there are
people who care.

I know I have
the right to live.
I know I'm fine
and know how to give.

No matter
what is the hold,
I can conquer it,
brave and bold.

The secret is
I start today,
as tomorrow
may be far away.

Autumn Leaves

The sun is rising
on a late autumn day.
Soon the world
is going to be ok.

With the colourful leaves
sailing off the branches,
it is sealed;
we are making advances.

Whatever harshness,
pain and doom,
it's the falling of the leaves,
completed so soon.

And after
one frosty winter night,
the sun will come up,
shining strong and bright.

With the powerful energy
taken from each morning's rise,
we'll be ready again
though much more wise.

And once the spring of our life
settles in again,
we'll have the strength to conquer the pain and hurt
that's done by man.

Only days later,
we won't even know,
we're back, full of life,
ready to go.

Bright and shiny
like the sun,
we are strong and committed,
giving life another run.

One thing though
we'll never forget
is to learn from mistakes,
from hurt and regret.

Mist

The morning mist
white land surrounds,
covering the soil
and all the grounds.

Just like clouds
covering our brain's folds,
a misty cover,
thick, it holds.

Lifting the mist
inside the head
rewards the mind,
with clear thoughts ahead.

Although the beauty
is in the mist,
a clear mind
will persist.

Just like
the mist's 'clearing ups,'
we can find ways
out of life's traps.

Heaven Is Here

Where no soul
is around,
where the noises
subside,

where nature
is present
and
trees and birds
reside,

no human
distraction
and no energy
spoiled,

that's where heaven lies.

Lost – Matters

Scared – why?
Lost – cry?

Now – too soon?
Space – no room?

Soul – gone?
What – strong?

Death – near?
Future – here?

What – loom?
See – doom?

Nowhere here
any fear.

Chapter 13
Esteem The Self

Being Me

What's stopping me
from being me?
From facing life's challenges
and feeling free?

I'm not too weak
to care for me.
I'm strong enough
to live and be.

Put fears aside;
get off the hook.
Don't care
when other people look.

What matters
is my happiness,
although
I won't forget others, I guess.

My happiness, though,
is what counts.
Peace and happiness,
that's how my life grounds.

I love the bush,
going out to enjoy;
breathing and moving
is my life's joy.

Be me;
step out and let the world go.
Things and 'ego' –
I want to be a 'no.'

Help me
learn to do what's right
for my mind, both
day and night,

and for my body,
as it is
connected
to my life's bliss.

Thank you, Lord,
for me being me.
Thank you
for giving 'me' the opportunity.

Thank you
for my mind to be
gentle, open,
respectful, and free.

This is what
I enjoy in life;
be part of this world
and let it thrive.

Beautiful

I'm beautiful,
with my wonky eye,
even if
it makes other people cry.

I am
the prettiest thing,
although my nose
turns my face into a grin.

I'm the best runner
in the world,
though with every step
my legs badly hurt.

I'm most handsome
and attractive,
although to others my face lines
appear distractive.

What is beauty?
Where does it start?
As all goodness in the world –
all beauty – comes from the heart.

Who cares
about the outer look
when it's the inner part
that deserves the 'hook'?

Is It Me?

Doing
my best,
putting
it at rest.

Wondering,
is it me?
Why?
It doesn't agree?

Having looked
at each side of the coin,
being open
and trying to join.

Many times
asking for help,
polite and friendly,
till the core will melt.

Although taken advantage of
at every step, still
care and politeness
is not what you get.

It's business
that counts;
money,
as bad as it sounds.

Whoever
doesn't fit in,
just appears
to make people grim.

Living up
to the goal,
being friendly
as a whole,

wondering why try
to belong,
if the morals
are gone?

Giving up, though,
is a loss,
like giving pity
to the boss.

More important is
to give,
to raise the spirit –
and to live.

Make the world
a better place;
give sanity
some space.

No matter
how many times we fall, or
feel we're running
into a wall,

keep on going;
there's no need to duck,
even if we feel like
being hit by a truck.

As standing up for
the right grounds,
truly is
the bit that counts.

Women

Being a woman
is being strong, wild, adventurous,
and with pride – under the cover
where we hide.

Want it all, see the world,
love to love
(though prefer
life not too rough).

Prisoners
in daily routines;
who would have thought
of such a life, it seems?

Breaking out
is the goal;
being me
on a roll.

How on Earth
to command
if our lives are
in such demand?

Exploited, belittled,
not strong enough;
if you say a thing,
you come across rough.

Break it free,
the real you,
'cause that's the only way
to get through.

Move beyond
daily routines;
feel the happiness
following your dreams.

With just one life
in this world,
make sure
you'll be heard.

Use time
wisely enough;
it's not just you
taking it rough.

Raise your voice
and be strong,
as life too soon
will be gone.

Share the pain
but move along.
Make yourself
and others strong.

Being Beautiful

Beauty and happiness,
they're our goals.
Fearful and anxious,
the inner part holds.

Showing off
how beautiful we are,
but, round the corner,
more pretty they are.

Money's spent
in buying nice clothes,
all for show,
worried about the 'wows'!

How lucky is it to be born
pretty as it is.
Operations and make-up
enhance the bliss.

Being beautiful
and rich,
we think
is life's pitch.

Not so fast –
it may not be
life's beauty
in what you see.

Although money, and riches,
and showing-off laughter,
still appear
to be what we're after,

don't be fooled
by the glitter;
it only
makes our lives bitter.

Money, beauty, and riches
too often fail
and come with a
drug and alcohol tale.

What's the point of watching
beauty on the screen
when it's a tale
of cocaine?

What's the point
of making your heart hurt
by someone
wearing a pretty skirt?

As life's real beauty to see,
and for us to win,
only comes
from the beauty within.

Chapter 14

Creating A Better World

Being Special

Am I afraid
of dark and scary things?
Am I afraid
of what the future brings?

Do I accidentally
invade people's space?
Do I get upset
when others infringe my grace?

Do I need to
push myself to run?
Do I often think that
I'm the lazy one?

Do I want to be
better than 'Grace'?
Don't we all secretly
want to win the race?

Do I want
to be the best?
On the other hand,
don't I just want
some rest?

Do I find
I'm not perfect at all?
How many
mistakes made
can I recall?

Do I love
to be just me?
Feel the power
of being free?

Do I love
to have a chat?
With friends,
or people I just met?

Do I love
to see the sun?
I'm sure
I'm not the only one.

Am I chilly
in the cold?
Running to shade
during heatwave's hold?

Do I delight
in caring and giving?
I'm sure we all share
this aspect of living.

Do I hate
being upset?
Do I have
some regret?

Do I love
happiness and play?
Do I love
just floating in the bay?

Do I love
being loved by someone?
Do I love
to love another one?

Do I love
friends and family?
Am I upset
if we don't agree?

Do I love
many days in my life?
Do I hate other days,
when I struggle to 'survive'?

Do I love
to 'show off' me?
We are all that silly,
aren't we?

Do I argue
when someone steals my purse?
Do I whinge
when my tummy hurts?

All in all,
won't you agree,
there is no difference
between you and me?

The only speciality found,
maybe,
is the wisdom
that there is nothing
special about me.

Words

Never
enough time?
Or
do we feel too fine?

Never
enough said?
Too often
plenty to regret?

Forgotten?
Or just ignored?
Poisoned by anger?
Or just abhorred?

Misunderstandings
stop the appearing.
We often regret
but pretend we're not hearing.

Two simple words
change lives around.
Two simple words
can turn the world around.

Nothing difficult to say,
can't you see?
A simple 'Thank You' –
don't you agree?

Hit

It doesn't matter –
that's what we thought.
Thrown, the banana skin
that we just bought.

When it happened
it was fast;
a slip on a banana skin
some time in the past.

The broken bones
and broken neck –
not even time
for regret.

Ever since,
never off the chair I went,
all due to a banana skin
that was never meant.

Careless, we go through
our every day,
until we get hit ourselves
along the way.

Careless is how
we walk through this world,
not realising
we might ourselves get hurt.

The skin we threw
might come back
in some way
we least expect.

Awareness
of our moves and acts
may save lives
along our tracks –

as perhaps, one day,
we may be sorry for the loss
from the banana skin
we toss.

Angel

We believe in God
and pray on our knees,
hoping
to put our lives at ease.

What is it, though,
that makes us strong?
Our belief is right?
All others are wrong?

Killing
in the name of God?
Don't you agree
this sounds very odd?

Sitting in church
and praying for the sin,
when on the way out
we make the next one begin?

Living life in the name of God
but not able to permit
another race or colour
to fit in it?

Believe
for all mankind to pray –
but don't include
the one who's gay?

Pray
for others to shine bright –
but only if they do
what *we* think is right?

Praying for others,
don't you agree,
is, many times,
simply praying for 'me'?

'Holy money' –
how does that sound?
In the end it's too often
the fortunes that count.

Don't we all
love to pray
for the world
to go 'my way'?

In this case,
don't we mostly forget
to pray against cruelty
for all creatures, I bet?

Even though,
it does sound odd
to pray for love
but fib to God?

What is the point
to pray for love and such kind
if it's not
on our true mind?

It is our heart
that tells the tale,
letting us know
we are on the right trail.

For most of us, though,
it is forgotten
to listen to our heart
that tells us what's rotten.

Believe in the 'Good'
and our soul –
isn't that
everyone's goal?

If you think
about the latter,
does the name
'God' here really matter?

Maybe
a better way to win
is to believe and follow
the 'Angel' within.

How To Stop A Giant

Is it truly what it seems?
A tiny virus shattering our dreams?
Life on Earth changed for good,
a reason unreal or misunderstood?

A great force behind the scene?
Using us, and very keen?
Freedom gone for us all?
A giant creating a new wall?

A wall for all
where we find
imprisonment
for all humankind?

A slave to a giant
we helped to build
with no remorse, compassion,
or guilt?

A giant taking life
from us all?
An open mind, though,
may stop our fall.

Letting Me Be

Life is easy,
can't you see?
Sit down
and just agree.

Life is made
for each one of us 'nuts,'
even if it seems to rip apart
our guts.

As each time
it feels the yearning,
there's an opportunity
for learning.

Thank you, Lord,
for what you gave to me:
a mind,
clear, respectful, and free;

a mind
that lets me be just me.
Thank you, Lord,
for letting me be.

Chapter 15

Something Beautiful To Share

What's Love

Thank you
for what you've given me:
to show my feelings
and set them free.

Teaching me
to share my thought
with no shame,
never fought.

Teaching me
to learn to listen
as it's more important
than kiss'n.

Teaching me
the little things:
of mountains high
and butterfly wings.

Teaching me
to be grateful for each day
as it soon
will pass away.

Teaching me
to be kind,
no matter
to whose person's mind.

Teaching me
to say 'hello'
to the stranger
on the go.

Showing gratitude
to life,
telling the truth to others
and helping them thrive.

Teaching me
to give respect,
no matter
what others might expect.

Teaching me
how life can be
very different
for you and for me.

Teaching me
that what I think,
is different to you –
may even
take you to the brink.

Teaching me
to listen carefully,
so that the mind
can be open and truly free.

Teaching me
to not assume,
but to listen to
how you see the moon.

Teaching me
to appreciate life
in all its beauty,
and to share it, to thrive.

Life's Bliss

Kangaroo on the hill,
the morning mist,
every day again –
that's life's bliss.

Dark clouds
are inviting to enjoy the rain.
Every moment of sunshine
enriches the brain.

Love the thunder, hear it
crash the air –
it means I'm alive
and allowed to care.

Care for myself
and the world around.
Care for
any movement and sound.

Care for
being part of this world.
Care for sharing
where no one gets hurt.

Kangaroo on the hill,
the morning mist,
every day again –
that's life's bliss.

Prayer

Let me listen;
let me grow.
Let me be
part of life's flow.

Let me hear
the inner voice;
let me follow
its guide and choice.

Let me be myself
and choose
my own way,
nothing to lose.

Let me hear
the peace inside;
let me follow
its love and guide.

Let me be
one with me.
Let me be honest, aware,
and free.

Let me feel
compassion inside.
Let me feel the love
and follow its guide.

Let me forgive
what I can't change.
Give me the strength
to change what's in range.

Let me be a tool
for the good,
knowing a better world
comes from the root,

as I can gain the strength
for life's ride
only from listening
to the good inside.

Gone Today Tomorrow

The darkest clouds,
where are they from?
Life should be nice
but the illusion's gone?

Focus here;
now is the time.
We can still survive
and make the world shine.

Live and give,
that's not too much.
Live your life
every day as such.

Life is precious
as, for everyone,
at any moment,
it may be gone.

Focus on love
every day,
for the future
as if to pray.

Live life now
and plan today,
for tomorrow is
a long way away.

And

And is a word
that doesn't make sense.
Or, perhaps
on the other hand,

it is one of the words
we simply can't miss.
As otherwise,
Love and Passion
would not exist.

Acknowledgements

I would like to thank the following for their brilliant work and inspiration:

Roger French / The Natural Health Society of Australia
https://www.health.org.au

Robyn Chuter – Empower Total Health
https://robynchuter.substack.com
https://empowertotalhealth.com.au

Greg Fitzgerald / Health For Life
https://healthforlife.com.au
https://healthforlife.com.au/blog

R Blank / Shield Your Body
https://www.shieldyourbody.com

I'm also extremely thankful to everyone who loved and supported my 1st book
Think Smart & Lose Weight & 'Sandy's Smart Weight Loss Blog'

Lastly, I would love to give my special thanks to:

My wonderful friends,
My Mum,

and much Trouble in Life.

About The Author

A German native and now Australian citizen, Sandy Bröcking is a devoted, loving, now retired nurse, after working for more than 17 years in various hospitals, countries and diverse intensive care units across the world.

These days Sandy is a winning author and inspiring presenter who has translated years of experiences and much observation into easy, dedicated, loving and challenging ways to share and master our 21st century life.

Sandy is dedicated to making the world a better place for all to live, share, survive, and thrive in and throughout our troubled 21st century.

A keen and passionate achiever, Sandy's first book, *Think Smart & Lose Weight*, was highly promoted and reviewed as the 'easiest book to read ever' and 'a testament of what is achievable'. Apart from her love of nature, good health and animals, Sandy is a keen cyclist and bushwalker, and enjoys exploring Australia.

www.ingramcontent.com/pod-product-compliance
Lightning Source LLC
Chambersburg PA
CBHW072001290426
44109CB00018B/2096